A Cup Of Miracles

Writing and Photography
by Emilie Lancour

ISBN: 978-1-7346723-3-6 (paperback)
Printed in the United States of America

Books by Emilie Lancour

It's Okay to be Okay;
Finding Joy through Grief

A Cup of Miracles

I dedicate this book to all who have believed
in my miracles and share their own with me.

*"The report of this miracle swept
through the entire countryside."*

Matthew 9:26 - NLT

Table of Contents

Introduction

Throughout my life, I have always felt a connection to God. My faith has helped me survive some really hard and awful times in my life. I start my day reading a couple of different devotions and recording my gratitude. I update a prayer list daily with new asks and check off those answered. I read the Bible and listen to a podcast. I attend Mass in a church building. I often pray the rosary as a way to relax and feel peace. I also meditate both with breathing techniques and with prayer. I receive healings each month and during those, I often connect to a scene from the Bible or feel the presence of Mother Mary. I do yoga sometimes with prayers and sometimes in silence. In all of this though, I am closest to God at the shores of Lake Superior. Here I can just be.

I taught in a special education classroom for 20 years before moving to an intermediate school district where I work closely with special education teachers and staff. I watched miracles happen every day with the students I had. I watched them learn about themselves and become confident and independent. I learned from them that it is a strength to ask for and accept help. I realized how little control we have over our lives and those around us.

My faith life became a huge part of my life once I started dating Steve. I became active in my church and we raised our boys in the faith. I taught high school Sunday school and the students often asked me how I knew there was a God. My answer was some of the miracles I share in this book. I ask them to reflect and think about things that happen to them or around them that they can not explain.

Getting pregnant and giving birth three times is a true miracle and my absolute favorite way God expresses love to us. My oldest is married and lives down the block. My middle is figuring out what to do now that he is done with high school. I decided last spring to homeschool my youngest. Some days it has been hard to get out of bed but my boys have kept me going because I know they need me. God entrusted me to be their mom and I know that even when it seems impossible, God knew what He was doing when He gave them to be to care for and love.

My faith was tested a lot in 2010. One of my best friends, Tacy, did not wake up from a nap in January. My husband's grandmother died in July. Then, my aunt, Blanche passed away in December from a brain tumor. We lost many others that year too. I was working with a counselor and relying on my faith, friends, and family to get through the days.

Introduction

In the fall of 2014, I was again meeting with a counselor. Through divine intervention, I was able to reconnect with my birth father, Bruce, after about three years of not communicating. I was able to hear some answers from him before he passed away in January of 2015. There were many signs related to this situation that reminded me that I am not in control of my life and that I need to trust God's plan.

One of my biggest moments of faith and experiencing miracles came in December of 2017. My husband Steve was recovering at home from minor surgery. All was well when I left in the morning but by that afternoon he was gone. I became a widow and single mom in an instant. My faith was one of the main ways I healed and have grown in this new way of life. I also relied on family, friends, journaling, healings, and physical connections to my body like massage, acupuncture, myofascial release, and chiropractic and I was on antidepressants. I used my journal writing to tell my story of finding joy while grieving in a self-published memoir. The miracles I witnessed and the signs I still receive give me hope that I too will be a guardian angel and watch over my loved ones.

Fast forward four years. I am in a relationship with a man named Chris. Our pasts are filled with many connections, but we did not know each other. We went to the same small high school two grades apart. I was on the swim team with one of his sisters. I remember his parents from the church we both attended. He had played hockey with my late husband when they were kids. My father-in-law was the loan officer that helped with his mortgage. My sister was connected with all three of his sisters. His brother had worked on my boat. His sister-in-law was a paraprofessional in my classroom for over ten years. I felt an instant connection to him the day we met.

Last year before Christmas, I subscribed to receive encouraging messages daily. When I heard the following message, I knew I needed to include it in this book.

Adapted from "Serendipity, Synchronicity, Signs, and Support." By Lisa Almquist; December 17, 2022

I want to talk about serendipity, synchronicity, sighs, and support. So, what is serendipity? Serendipity is something that happens seemingly by chance, that has a happy result. What is synchronicity? Synchronicity is something that happens when you really step back and you look at it, you are like," Yeah that didn't just happen by chance"; that was the cause, effect, a gift from above. What's a sign? A sign is evidence from the universe and communication from the Universe; from God, that your serendipities and synchronicities are actually true.

You will experience so much greater joy, peace, and clarity if you slow down enough to notice where the serendipities, synchronicities, and signs are. Evidence starts to come through in random events that seem to just kind of happen and it all works out in the end. When you let go of the control of how something must go, it opens you into the flow of the Divine. So, the more you surrender and trust in that flow, the more you will be reminded that peace, clarity, and joy are available to you, but you've got to choose it. And you choose it by trusting that the present moment you are in, is perfect.

Your spirit guides are with you all the time, waiting to communicate with you. Here's a way to call in that support: "I call on the energy of Christ to support me to honor and love myself as He has loved me." How beautiful is that?! Connect to your spirit guides, connect to Jesus, to the energy of Christ Consciousness. Look for the serendipities, the synchronicities, and the signs and call on the support that is all around you to help you tap into the flow, experience more peace and more joy, and trust the process as it unfolds.

I hope that by reading my experience with miracles, signs, and connections to God, you will be able to witness more of your own. May God bless you with His love and signs. May His guardian angels continue to watch over you and let you know they are there. I designed the last few pages of this book so you are able to record the miracles you experience.

Chapter 1

Music

Instead, be filled with the Holy Spirit, singing psalms and hymns and spiritual songs among yourselves, and making music to the Lord in your hearts.

Ephesians 5:18-19

When I was driving around in another town at a spot that Steve always went to, two songs that reminded me of him came on the radio. One of the same ones played the next time I was there too.

The description for an 80's rock ballads playlist on Amazon is, "Wherever you go, whatever you do, your favorite 80's rock ballads will be right here waiting for you." Of the 100 songs on the playlist, they chose to adapt lyrics from Richard Marx's "Right Here Waiting"...my song with Steve.

One day I was listening to a song by Adele. There was an ad about her touring when I switched radio stations.

Music

"Amazing Grace" started to play when I was writing the dedication page in my memoir. This song is one I sang to my boys to help them sleep. It has been played at many funerals for loved ones.

One evening my son was wearing his sunglasses even though it was fairly dark outside. The song playing on the radio when we got in the car was, "I Wear My Sunglasses at Night".

Pulling into the church I was thinking about what it's like to be in heaven and a song was playing on the radio that was from that perspective.

A Cup of Miracles

Our friend Michelle always thinks of Steve when she hears the song "November Rain". I heard it one day and sent her a message. She opened the message while she was waiting at a Tiger's game. Steve was a huge Detroit Tigers baseball fan.

When Steve and I got married we stayed in a cabin and listened to Bob Seger CDs. I attended a Garth Brooks concert and one of the songs he played at the end was a Bob Seger song. I had also found a quarter while I was waiting in line to have my bag checked.

Chapter 2

Time and Dates

"However, no one knows the day or hour when
these things will happen, not even the angels in
heaven or the Son himself. Only the Father knows."

Matthew 24:36 NLT

A Cup of Miracles

A friend told me that she always saw 11:11 and that it was a sign from her godmother who had passed away. I see 11:11 most days, sometimes both in the morning and at night. One night a candle turned on and I looked to see what time it was and it was 11:11. Another day we were traveling and because of the time change, I got to see it three times.

I often see numbers on the clock that are repeating such as 4:44. Sometimes these are called angel numbers. One morning I was awake to use the bathroom at 2:22 and when I went to lunch with a friend she happened to make a note on her phone and it was also 2:22. A lady from my church said she says a prayer every time she sees the repeating numbers.

I was riding up a hill and saw an eagle. I asked Chris to pull over. As we stopped the eagle landed on the top of an old building. Perfect timing.

Time and Dates

My son noticed a license plate on the car ahead of us. It said DEC 1946. He commented that maybe it was the year the person driving had been born. It's the year and month my father-in-law was born.

I was thinking about writing a book about my grief journey and heard about an organization called Hope Writers. When I called them to see about the details, they told me that that was the last day of open enrollment. They only have open enrollment a couple of times a year for short periods.

When I was young my sister said I was talking in my sleep and said something like "bonzo" and "twelve twelve". I always think about her when I see 12:12.

A Cup of Miracles

My mom and a friend both talked to me about the same book on the same day. On another day I received two different email subscriptions talking about books by the same author.

Steve taught in a middle school and I happened to talk to the secretary on the same day that she received a piece of mail addressed to him. She said it was the first piece of mail she had gotten in about three years.

Steve passed away on December 19th, 2017. I started dating Chris on September 19th, 2020. It has helped me feel very loved on the 19th of each month.

Time and Dates

My oldest son proposed to his girlfriend on April 20th. This was the anniversary of the first time Steve and I went on a date 27 years before.

Chris and I were riding down a small side road and talking about how his mom had needed tennis balls put on the bottom of her walker. Right on the road was a tennis ball. Neither of us could believe that we were seeing it.

I often drive my car and don't remember driving most of the trip. Since I arrived safely, I assume someone is watching over me.

A Cup of Miracles

One fall, Steve told me that he wanted something other than sandwiches in his lunches. I came up with the idea of pasties. I decided to make my grandma's recipe and knew my aunt had it. I kept thinking of calling her but thought of it at random times that were either not convenient or I did have her phone number with me. I decided I would make them the weekend before Thanksgiving and I called her, she gave me the recipe, we talked for a while, and then she said she was glad I had called because she felt my birth father, Bruce, needed to go to the hospital but wouldn't go. He could barely walk and was in pain. She felt I should call him and tell him to go to see a doctor. I told her I wasn't sure I could do that. I hadn't talked to him in three years and was seeing a counselor trying to figure out our relationship, but I would pray about it. I called my best friend who told me I needed to figure out the answers myself and that she could not tell me what to do. I asked her, "What if he dies and I do not know the answers to my questions?". I needed to know why he had signed away his parental rights when I was little. She told me that was my answer. I called him the next morning and talked to him for about 45 minutes. He told me he signed the parental rights papers because he loved me and that it was the hardest decision he ever had to make but knew I had a really good life. We both cried.

Time and Dates

I opened a package in the mail to find a pair of toe socks with flying pigs on them from my friend Kendra. Tacy loved wearing toe socks and also loved flying pigs. While I was looking at them my phone notified me that I had received a text from Tacy's husband. I have not heard from him for quite a while.

While I was a middle school special ed teacher, I was feeling bad about not reaching students and questioned if I was doing the right thing with the students. On the way home from parent-teacher conferences, I felt the need to stop by the grocery store. I met a mom there who gave me a big hug and told me that her daughter wasn't sure that the co-teaching was going to go well at the start of the year, because she wasn't one of "my kids" but now her daughter is doing great and attributes her success and self-confidence to me. She said I am so good at what I do. I emailed her the next day and told her how I was meant to meet her that night and she replied with the same thing. She had thought of emailing me a couple of times but hadn't and when she saw me she was overwhelmed with the need to let me know.

One evening I happened to look out my kitchen window and could tell the sunset was going to be gorgeous. I can not see that part of the sky from my house so I decided to grab my camera, drive to a park and take pictures. I learned the next morning that a friend of mine, Julie, had passed away at that same time. The sun was setting over the end-of-life place she was staying at. I have since shared pictures with her family. I know it as a sign that she had made it to heaven. (The picture from that night is the cover photo.)

One morning, I was working with a brand new special education teacher and she was teasing me about being quizzed on acronyms as I wasn't sure what one stood for. That afternoon, during a webinar I was watching, there was an acronym quiz. I did well because I had looked up a couple during our conversation.

Time and Dates

I play Bingo from my local newspaper. The new card comes at the end of the month. I realized that the serial numbers on the two cards I was playing that month were consecutive. One of the cards had come from Chris and one had come from my mother-in-law. They do not live close by or have similar names for the mailing of the paper.

One morning at 6:15 my cousin's power steering went on the school bus she was driving. . She pulled over and called the mechanic. By 6:40, the bus was on fire. If the power steering had not gone out when it did she would have four kids on the bus. No one was injured.

Chapter 3

Money

"Then a poor widow came by and dropped in two small coins."

Luke 21:2 NLT

A Cup of Miracles

Steve leaves me quarters all over the place. Only a single quarter. The first one was on the running board of my truck. It stayed for months. I have found others, in my bed, on the couch, by the snow pile, on the beach, in my medicine cabinet, in a basket by my bed, on the table in my basement, in the washing machine, in the bottom of my purse, under the table at a restaurant, on a friend's kitchen counter while making breakfast, on my TV stand in my bedroom, in the seal on the door of my truck, under a milk jug during dinner at his parent's house, and once one fell out of my truck as I opened the door.

A friend of mine, Lacey, called to tell me that she was at a football game and after heading towards the field, she placed her purse on a bleacher. When she picked up her purse, there was a quarter there. She picked it up and realized it was an Arizona quarter. When she called me, she said she knew Steve was watching over us because not only was it a quarter but because it had Arizona on it. My son and I had taken a trip to Arizona together the summer after Steve died. I had found a quarter in my bed the same day as the football game. I picked it up off my nightstand and it also was an Arizona quarter.

Money

Lacey also traveled to a spot in Florida where my kids and I had gone a few months before. When she got there a quarter fell out of her suitcase. When she was at the front desk, there was a penny in the jar of bracelets. She messaged me to tell me that she loves knowing we are being watched over.

When visiting Steve's tombstone at the cemetery I left a quarter there and it was still there in the same spot over a year later.

Lacey knows her grandpa leaves small piles of coins for her, usually dimes, nickels, and pennies. The day after I heard this I was returning to my car from an appointment and there on the ground was a pile of coins. I knew her grandpa was watching over me that day.

While walking on the beach one morning at sunrise I found a penny in the sand on my way back to my car. I had not noticed it on my way down the beach. (The picture of the penny is the back cover photo.)

The following is an email exchange between a member of my church and myself. I was fundraising for an orphanage in Uganda to provide them with water tanks. I had spoken in front of the congregation that we needed $2500 more to meet the goal. After the service, this woman gave me a check for $2500 in honor of her mom. I emailed her:

"I can not tell you what the honoring of your mom meant yesterday. I could not believe it. It was perfect!!! We were so close to reaching the goal and I was trying to figure out what to do without another fundraiser. I was praying for an idea of how to raise the rest of the money and you called my name! I was ready to head home and brainstorm. With your donation, we have the perfect amount to end phase 1!!! We are now able to start construction of the tanks! Father contacted the priest at the Diocese in Uganda and the contractors will start as soon as possible. Your mom is smiling down on you!"

Here is part of the letter I got back:

"THANK YOU and "we" are so happy phase 1 can begin!!! I was thinking of making a large donation in memory of my mom and actually, that was the amount I was thinking- then you made that announcement in church for that exact amount needed and I felt like it was a sign. My mom LOVED children and was sooooo good to her grand"babies" as she lovingly called them, from the oldest to the youngest. I had recently learned of a small annuity my mom had and received checks from it. I hadn't cashed mine yet as I wanted to do something special with the money. Your amazing caring program seemed like the PERFECT gift from/ to my mom. Emilie, we are humbled by all you (and your family) do for the church day in and day out - and this amazing project is just way above and beyond. My mom also gave so much of her life to her church and to help others - so I was happy and honored to do this in her memory. She is happy I'm sure- but more importantly- she would hope the "children" feel a loving comforting "hug" in their hearts from her and ALL the strangers who have reached out to help them."

A Cup of Miracles

One day I went to pay a friend. When I checked my checking account balance, I had the exact amount that I owed her.

My middle son and a friend were bartenders for a wedding. They had a tip jar. Someone needed a dollar so they gave one from the jar. At the end of the night, they counted the money. It was $150, but it was more perfect than just $75 each. In the bottom of the jar were two gold dollar coins. One for each. As they divided the rest of the cash they realized that all of the denominations were equal as well. There were two twenties, two tens, ten fives, and a bunch of ones.

While waiting for my myofascial release appointment to start, my therapist and I were standing by her counter. I noticed a quarter under the edge of a book. When I picked it up she asked where it came from. She had just set the book down and there was not a quarter.

My daughter-in-law sent me a text: "I told Kiwi (their dog) 'I wish something could give a sign that I am making the right choice'. I get to your house, I'm picking out my cup and getting ready to grab my chai to put next to the cup and I found a quarter. The quarter wasn't there yesterday." When I told her it was from Steve, her response was, "It's not the first time I've found one when I'm having a hard day or when I just need something. I usually don't think anything of it because it always seemed weird to me that he would watch over me when he didn't know me that well."

Chapter 4

Nature

"When I send clouds over the earth,
the rainbow will appear in the clouds."

Genesis 9:14 NLT

A Cup of Miracles

I always feel close to God when I am watching a sunrise or a sunset. It makes my breath slow, my shoulders relax and a feeling of peace comes over me.

I took a ride one day to a place where Steve had gone fishing. It was a cloudy, foggy day. When I got to the dock, the fog lifted for a few minutes as if he was saying hi.

Driving down a hill a week or so after Tacy had passed away I saw a rainbow...but it was winter so I decided that it must be a snowbow. It is the only time I have ever seen a rainbow in February.

Nature

My grandpa collected rocks called Omars when I was little. My Grandma taught me how to pick agates. Now when I go to the beach at their camp, I find at least one of each every time.

During the first winter while in deep grief I would have a hard time getting out of bed. On these days I would hear an owl. I felt like it was telling me that I would be okay. I heard that a snowy owl had been seen in my neighborhood.

I was talking to another teacher who taught in a district about 20 miles north of me. Our conversation was discouraging and I said, "at least the sun is shining". She told me it was cloudy and gray there. I jokingly said I would send some her way and I got an email about 20 minutes later telling me, "thank you for sending the sunshine". I wish I had sent it sooner.

I was walking down on the beach by the water's edge. On my return, I noticed another set of footprints by mine although no one else was on the beach. Then the two sets of footprints merged into one for about 10 steps and then went back to being two sets. I felt Jesus telling me that when I need him to, He will carry me. It reminds me of the poem, "Footprints in the Sand".

Chris bought his mom a rose bush each year for Mother's Day. This past spring in honor of her memory I bought him a rose bush and he planted it at his family's camp. In October, his family and I were there doing cleanup of leaves and putting away everything. On the hillside the rose bush was in full bloom. We all felt their mom was with us.

Nature

After Steve had died, a friend would drive four hours to visit me once a month. Every trip, she saw a rainbow.

Chapter 5

Faith

"God works in different ways, but it is the same God who does the work for all of us. A spiritual gift is given to each of us so we can help each other. To one person the Spirit gives the ability to give wise advice; to another, the same Spirit gives a message of special knowledge. The same Spirit gives great faith to another, and to someone else the one Spirit gives the gift of healing. He gives one person the power to perform miracles, and another the ability to prophesy. He gives someone else the ability to discern whether a message is from the Spirit of God or from another spirit."

1 Corinthians 12:1-31 NLT

A Cup of Miracles

One of my first very religious miracles was while attending an anniversary Mass for my aunt and uncle at a different church than my normal parish. When I went to communion, I looked at the bottom of the chalice and there was a heart. I wasn't sure if it was part of the metal or not. I wondered about it but didn't say anything. The next week I was at my church and saw three intertwined rings at the bottom of the chalice. I again wondered if it was the lighting or what could cause this. I have experienced the three rings almost every time I receive communion or provide it to others as a Eucharistic Minister regardless of where I am standing or how much wine is in the chalice. I feel it is the trinity: God, Jesus, and the Holy Spirit. Catholics believe that the wine becomes the blood of Jesus. I know of another two people who have also witnessed the rings.

Sitting in church on Saturday night, I have my hands folded in front of me and as I look at them, two marks look like doors to me on the sides of my thumbs. I opened my hands and heard God speak to me. He says " I have opened the doors for you. It is your choice to go through them or not."

Faith

Often when I meditate about being a mother and how I am raising my boys, I feel like I am being touched and watched by Mother Mary. I heard her tell me once that she raised Jesus without Joseph and that I could raise my boys without Steve.

One of the stories I often told the Sunday School students was when my husband's grandfather died. He was placed on a ventilator until the family could get to the hospital to decide what to do. The family knew he would not want to live that way and we gathered in his hospital room to say goodbye. The nurse turned off the ventilator and told us he would slowly stop breathing. We all stood at his bedside and his wife asked that we pray the rosary. She took two out of her purse and put one under his hand and one in hers. I watched the heart monitor during this time and the moment we finished the last prayer, the line went flat and he took his last breath. I know he was waiting and praying with her one last time.

A Cup of Miracles

My friend Kris gave me a small metal disc called "a pocket angel" on a day I was having a hard time. She said she had been meaning to give it to me for a few days but kept forgetting. It had been 10 months since Steve had passed away.

I have three beautiful boys. They are a miracle. The whole idea of conception and birth is miraculous. When Michael was a baby (and somewhat for the other two) I would be so tired that I could barely stay awake to sing a lullaby. I would place a cross on his forehead and pray to my grandpa (who had just passed away) for him to watch over Michael and help him sleep. Almost always, Michael fell asleep quickly and would sleep through the night. There are guardian angels. I believe that my grandpa died so Michael could come to be. It is a full circle.

Faith

In January of 2015, I learned that my birth father, Bruce, was admitted to the hospital with bladder and bone cancer. Once we made it to the hospital many hours away, my aunt, cousin, Bruce's girlfriend, and I met with the social worker. They were arguing over where he was going to spend his remaining time. That night, I wrote a letter about my feelings to give to the social worker as I knew I would not be able to talk about it without getting upset but I felt he needed to stay there. That next morning one of the Bible verses was "My body hurts and my bones ache. Please Lord take me to be with you". I knew it was a sign. When we got to the hospital, the doctor came to talk with us about hospice. Bruce was back on a ventilator as his breathing had gotten worse during the night and if they remove the ventilator, he will pass away. We all agree as he was in so much pain. As we gathered around the bed; we sang "Amazing Grace"; told him we loved him and that he was free to go when he was ready; and that we would be okay. We played music including "In the Garden" which was one of my gramma's favorites and also his. He very slowly stopped breathing. His heart stopped. He was gone. I was so thankful that God had connected us in November.

Before Easter one year, I was reflecting on the gospel readings and I suddenly felt a pain-like feeling in my lower right abdomen. I know this is where Jesus was pierced when he was on the cross.

My morning routine includes reading a devotional, a passage from a spiritual book, writing in my journal, and filling out my bullet journal with what I hear God saying to me each morning. Many mornings, all of these things are connected and have the same topic.

Since 2016, I have chosen word of the year during December. My word for the year 2020 was going to be confidence. When

Faith

I attended Mass on the first Sunday in January the sermon was about confidence confirming that my choice was correct.

Chapter 6

People

"'In the last days,' God says, 'I will pour out my Spirit upon all people. Your sons and daughters will prophesy. Your young men will see visions, and your old men will dream dreams.'"

Acts 2:17 NLT

A Cup of Miracles

I was talking with a friend of mine who lost a baby because of trisomy 18 and asked if she had resources because my sister's friend also lost a baby for the same reason. She gave me the resource and I passed it on to my sister. Turns out the two friends know each other.

- The resource is called "The trisomy 18 Foundation"

I was sharing with my friend and co-worker, Andrea, how I feel I am meant to share my grief and healing story to help others. I mentioned that another teacher connected me with his sister when her husband passed away. Andrea grew up down the street from the teacher and his sister in a town about 2 hours away.

A six-year-old girl connected to my daughter-in-law was diagnosed with stage 4 brain cancer around Thanksgiving time. Her test results the following March came back clear with no signs of cancer.

People

I was telling my sister that a counselor I had met with in the past had once told me that if we saw each other in public that she would never initiate a conversation and not to be rude but because of confidentiality. If I started the conversation, she was happy to talk. I ran into this counselor the next day. I have not seen her for many years and we had an amazing conversation (that I started).

When I decided to start dating again, I noticed that someone named Chris was liking my photos on Facebook. I asked him if he picked agates and he said no. I offered to teach him how that coming Saturday as the weather was supposed to be nice. There's no date of when our friendship on Facebook started. But I felt an immediate connection to him when we met. We agreed to go out to dinner a couple of days later. So many of our hobbies and interests match. We have now been together for a year and a half.

A Cup of Miracles

Chris and I were talking about how my mom was out running errands at the same time we were and about how traffic was crazy. When we pulled up to the intersection my mom was going in the opposite direction.

Because both my husband and I had been teachers, my son was hoping to date someone that had not been in the classroom with either one of us. He started dating a girl who neither of us knew. We then realized that her mom had taken care of my grandma for many years in a nursing home, my sister had done a skincare class for her when she was a teenager and I had had her uncle as a student one of my first years of teaching.

People

While visiting a beach, I took a picture of another photographer. He was laying in the sand with huge waves and a lighthouse behind him. I decided to show him the picture. He recognized me as a teacher from the school he had attended many years ago.

I was out of town (four hours away) and stopped at a local store and when I was asked if I needed a gift receipt, I mentioned that I wasn't local and wouldn't be able to return the item. She inquired where I was from and when I told her where she said that she and her family had just vacationed here at a local set of cabins. I told her that I knew the owners of the cabins. In addition to that, I contacted my friend who owns the cabins and it reminded me that I was supposed to have another marketing session with her.

My friend Jen was having a lot of difficulties getting pregnant. She and her husband were not from here. She was working with medical professionals and having to take time off to go hours away to her appointments. But, once her family moved out of the area and was close to both families and near a medical center, she got pregnant and gave birth to a boy.

Another friend has a tumor in her head. Once finding out that it was not cancerous, she stopped having headaches and was able to conceive. She too gave birth to a boy. She also had been trying for many years to conceive.

My sister and brother-in-law grieved through many miscarriages over six years and then she gave birth to a boy. Although she struggled with illness during her pregnancy, he did not need any support at birth. He was born during the pandemic and the visitor restrictions were changed a day or two before his birth so we were able to see him in the hospital. Her health improved with the delivery. Both are doing great!

People

While driving one day, I was thinking about a family friend that Chris had just lost. I wasn't sure if I should say something or not. Right then, Chris told me a story about her.

I was at Steve's parent's house and my friend Karen sent me a text to watch the graduation ceremony of the school where Steve taught. We open the youtube link on the TV. One of the valedictorians cries as he talks about the difference that Steve made in his life. He talked about Steve being someone who believed in him and had high expectations for him. He also said that when he was in 6th grade, Steve was one of the only people who believed that he would someday own a corvette. The next morning I am driving by the school and see a young man standing by a corvette in the parking lot. I learn later that it was most likely him because he owns and drives a white corvette.

Chapter 7

Guardian Angels

*"And in this fellowship, we enjoy
the eternal life he promised us."*

1 John 2:25 NLT

A Cup of Miracles

Tara, the mom of one of my son's friends, was driving by my house and saw an ambulance the day Steve died. She felt the need to stop and pray with whoever was there. She prayed with my in-laws and then followed them to the hospital. She was able to come and get me from my job and my boys from school so his parents and sister could be at the hospital. Tara was much-needed support that day and for the next couple of months. She was only driving by my house because there had been a snow day the week before and her bible study had been moved to this day. She was driving a friend home after the study who happened to live near me.

Steve's mom said a small prayer asking for confirmation that he was okay. A few minutes later, she found a child's block by her chair with the letter "S" on it.

Before Steve passed away we had had many conversations about what would happen if he was to pass away as far as life insurance, working, assets, debt, etc. I don't think we ever talked about what would happen if I passed away first. I think this was preparation for what I would have to deal with financially.

A single fruit fly appeared in strange places, such as on my ankle at the beach, on my bathroom counter, in my bed, at a restaurant, in a campground, while installing outlets at my son's house, at Steve's parent's house in the living room, and in my car. I am not sure why a fruit fly kept appearing, but it was a comfort to see.

Steve hated the fact that shower curtains would brush against him when he took a shower. He appreciated that sometimes hotels would have a curved rod so that didn't happen. When I was having a hard day or feeling a lot of grief, part of my shower curtain would move and stick to my leg. I know it is his way of saying that he is always by my side. It still happens four years later.

I have often heard that pennies are found and it is a sign that a loved one is watching over you. In June after Steve had died, a quarter fell on the running board of my vehicle. It was there for months and one day my mom commented that maybe Steve had sent it for me. He used to say. "Take this quarter and call someone who cares". I miss his sense of humor.

I was cleaning out the chest freezer in my basement to get rid of the rest of the funeral food that did not get eaten and in the very bottom corner was a single Hershey kiss.

My friend Kendra had a dream that Steve was talking to her and he was wearing a red Carhartt shirt. That shirt has never been found since his death. It makes me wonder if we wear clothes in heaven and if so, is that what he is wearing?

A 12-year-old son of a local teacher passed away very unexpectedly. The next Sunday in church, I could see Steve kneeling by a young boy. He told the boy, "Do you see that boy down there? That is my son Matthew. I watch over him like you are going to watch over your brother." I know that the boy in this vision was the boy who had passed away.

A few days before Steve's aunt passed away I was praying in church and the song "Amazing Grace" was being played on the piano. I immediately pictured Steve holding his aunt in a hug and swinging her legs back and forth like a bell. This was something he would do every time he saw her.

At my aunt's funeral, we were given a Peace Lily. I am not very good at keeping plants alive, but this plant would wilt, and I knew to water it and other plants I owned. I know my aunt was reminding me. I still have the plant because of her guidance.

I had spent a lot of time with Tacy during middle and high school. Her nickname in school was Just a Flying Pig...JFP for short. I was teaching a study hall class one day about a month after Tacy died and the student asked me if I would help him decide on a color to finish his art project. When he came back from his locker with the piece of paper it was a flying pig in bright orange, one of her favorite colors. Why would a teenage boy make an orange flying pig?

Our Goddaughter was riding in their van to take a vacation and she asked for the volume to be turned down on her iPad so she could hear Steve talking to her.

Fun patterned Lularoe leggings were very popular the year that Tacy died. I was able to get a pair with flying pigs on them. I wore them to my middle school teaching job and a student told me that my flying pigs were "fabulous"...a word that Tacy loved to use.

During Tacy's funeral, they played "How Great Thou Art". A few weeks later, I was playing it at home and my three-and--a-half-year-old said, "I know this song. It was from when we were at Tacy's church."

Chapter 8

Healings

"Stretch out your hand with healing power;
may miraculous signs and wonders be done
through the name of your holy servant Jesus."

Acts 4:30 NLT

A Cup of Miracles

Upon smelling the Harmony oil, I felt like I was in an old church. I was witnessing a woman down on one knee dropping coins into a copper bucket. The bucket was placed at the bottom of three stone tile-covered steps. My knee felt funny and I noticed that she had difficulty kneeling. I think when you brought your offering you were supposed to be down on both knees. But this woman was struggling. I then realized I was witnessing the widow dropping coins into the collection. I felt that when Jesus was telling the story it was because He had experienced it when He was young.

One time during a healing session, I smelled Valor oil and suddenly was witnessing Mary Magdalene putting oil on Jesus's feet.

I was spending some time in meditation and the music that was playing had small birds singing. I immediately felt that I was in the garden of Gethsemane on the morning that Judas brought people to take Jesus into custody. I could see there was a short rock wall around the garden area, the sun was shining and birds were singing. I could feel that Jesus was at peace even though He knew what was happening.

Another time during a healing meditation, my hand got very sore and I realized it was where Jesus was nailed to the cross.

A memory of my mom reading the book, "Blueberries for Sal", came to my mind. Thinking more about why I was shown a scene of a young boy and a mom on a hillside picking some sort of berries. I know it was Mary and Jesus when He was little. He kept eating the berries and when she asked Him how many He had picked, He performed a miracle and filled half of His bucket. It made her smile.

A Cup of Miracles

A few weeks after Steve had died I lay in my bed and had a conversation with Jesus. He told me to be a mom first and everything else will fall into place. To be present because time is more precious than anything you can buy. God said that he needed Steve to be with all the babies and children. He had told Steve that He was going to bring him home soon so that's why Steve had stopped being on some committees and had been spending more time with God. God told me to go with Michael, to take Matthew to a pool, and to be alone with Brian. I felt a quick pain in my side. God told me that that was where His side had been pierced when He was on the cross. He said that I was healed. That I could do this. That I didn't need Steve to be here with me to be happy. That I can be alone. During this experience, I could sense light coming from the left side of my room and I felt the need to hold both hands over my heart. I finally felt that I was hearing Jesus speak to me as a friend and not like God as I usually experienced. I have no idea how long I spent in prayer talking with Jesus, but it was incredible. He ended by telling me, "Don't worry about what others think. Do what is right for you and for the boys".

Healings

Praying during mass one Sunday, I heard Mary tell me that I can raise my boys alone because she raised Jesus alone after Joseph had died. I again saw the three entwined rings at the bottom of the chalice during communion.

Chapter 9

Others Experiences

"Who can list the glorious miracles of the LORD? Who can ever praise him enough?"

Psalm 106:2 NLT

A Cup of Miracles

These are stories based on posts from my friend Monica's blog. She and her husband Rob have experienced quite a lot of huge miracles.

"These are the MIRACLES that have occurred in my life - the examples of Divine Intervention that go beyond the ordinary."

After years of not getting pregnant, we tried science. Eventually, we heard that not a single one of those eggs were fertilized. It was a scenario that had never happened before in any of the specialist's knowledge. We were devastated. I felt so strongly called to be a mother, and yet it seemed the likelihood of that happening was quickly deteriorating. The day I was supposed to go for our last IVF treatment, I called the fertility clinic and told them that I wasn't able to start the drugs "on time", and requested a pregnancy test. The results? Pregnant. Unbelievable. Without fertility drugs, without the help of medical science. During my ultrasound, I was asked "did anyone tell you that this pregnancy was unusual?" I panicked immediately. WHAT WAS WRONG?? He showed me the baby; its sac; its heartbeat. Thank God. The baby was alright. Then he said "and here's the OTHER baby. You're having identical twins!" As if to leave no doubt about the nature of this amazing gift

God had blessed us with, the boys were born on my birthday. Happy Birthday to me, from God. I get to be a mom.

We knew before the boys were born that there was water on their kidneys. It was a difficult pregnancy, and the boys were born 6 weeks premature. We soon found out that each boy had a "dead" kidney, and would need it removed. That was scheduled soon after their first birthday. The surgeries were long but successful. For one twin there was an issue with the remaining kidney. If the reflux persisted uncorrected, he would most likely need a kidney transplant. For another year we watched him closely, had regular tests to assess the damage to his remaining kidney, and gave him daily medication. When visiting my parents, my mother asked if we could have our son anointed at church. I was skeptical but thought there was no reason not to. The priest called us up during the service – We were asked to lay our hands on him as the priest anointed him with oil and began praying. It was no ordinary prayer. Father Jack prayed under his breath, but I could tell it was not English he was speaking – he was praying in tongues. Our baby, surprisingly, fell immediately into a deep heavy sleep in Rob's arms. He didn't awaken for the entire rest of the service. Rob leaned over to me and said "something happened. I could feel it. He just went so instantly calm." A month later, it was time to have his annual kidney study done. The doctor started the procedure, and then asked me "What am I looking for again?" I told her grade V reflux. She was quiet. Then she said, "Well, I don't see anything." Nothing? Not at all??? "There's no reflux here." He was healed. Completely.

I felt enormously blessed by the gift of our sons, their miraculous entrance into our lives. I knew I wanted four kids, but I felt like we were only missing ONE – that, to me, was proof that my "feeling" wasn't of my origin. When the boys were two and a half, I was at work one day when a truly amazing thing happened. I was doing therapy with a 10-year--old autistic boy, when he suddenly stopped, looked at me, and said "Who's going to be my therapist when you have the baby?" I was shocked but said "I'm not having a baby. You don't have to worry about that." He was insistent, though, and very worried about who would be his therapist when the baby arrived. I tried to divert the conversation, thinking it was inappropriate. He would not be diverted. "I'm not having a baby." "Yes you are," he replied. "It's a girl. Monica Jr. She's standing there waving at me! See? She looks like you, and she'll be born in November." This was September when all of this occurred – further proof that this young man was just being silly. I couldn't shake the feeling that I was being spoken to by more than a 10-year-old boy. The next morning, I gave in and took a pregnancy test. I was, indeed, pregnant. This baby would be due in May. Late in October, I miscarried. The next time I saw him for therapy, he looked at me and said "Where'd the baby go? Is she born?" I told him she was up in Heaven. He just shrugged and said "Oh. She was supposed to be born in November." He never said another word about it. I was devastated once again, but felt guilty about my grief – how greedy was I to want more than what God had already granted me? After all, we'd been through with the boys? The feeling wouldn't go away, however, that someone was MISSING. I felt it so strongly, and yet Rob was adamant it was my DESIRE for another child talking, and not something more. Tension grew between us again. Finally, one day, Rob said "Fine. If you can get pregnant before you turn 35, I'll consider it. Otherwise, you need to give up this idea of another child forever."I knew my fertility was poor. We'd been married almost 10 years by that time, and I'd been successfully pregnant only once, despite being open to pregnancy for most of that time. So I prayed. I remember distinctly one day praying to Mary – something I am admittedly not in the habit of doing. I remember praying "Mary, you are a mother, and know the desires of a mother's heart. If you see fit to ask your son to bless us with another child, I would be truly thankful." That was it – my simple prayer. On Easter Sunday, 2 months before my 35th birthday, I gave in and took a pregnancy test - certain that it would be negative just as every other disappointing test had been before it. This time, however... It was positive! I was ecstatic!! How fitting to find out about new life on Resurrection Sunday!! Even more surprising, our first ultrasound showed us that we were having identical twins yet again. At 9 weeks, however, I lost one of the babies and was again on bed rest for a short time. That's when it occurred to me... I had always wanted four children but strongly felt like God only promised us ONE more. It helped me through that miscarriage, that promise. And despite early labor pains that threatened an early October delivery, we made it until NOVEMBER and gave birth to a baby GIRL. Just like my patient had said we would. Little girl, who looks a whole lot like her Mommy.

Our son unexpectedly launched into a long description of a recent dream that he had.

C: "Mom, I dreamt that we had two babies instead of one and that she was like you and was an identical twin.".

I stopped cold. What was he talking about?

Me: "So, this was your dream?"

C: "Yeah, but it seemed real. Not just like a dream. There were two babies, and they were identical and looked exactly alike, but one lived with us, and the other one lived in a house in the woods."

Me: "Was it me and Aunt Elle? People used to say we looked alike."

C: "No, it wasn't her. It was our baby that looked like you, and she had an identical twin, who lives in the woods now, in a house."

What C DOESN'T know, because I don't think we ever discussed it with him, and he was 3 years old when it happened, so he COULDN'T know (could he?) - is that our daughter was an identical twin, and we miscarried her sister early on in the pregnancy. We DID have "two babies", and one DOES live with us, and the other doesn't. The other thing that struck me is that he didn't say the baby was our daughter's name. He called her "the baby that looked like you". I felt like I was just wished a Happy Mother's Day from our little girl up in Heaven. Sweet girl. I can't wait to meet you someday.

A Cup of Miracles

Another friend was sharing miracles with me when I was telling her about my book almost being ready to publish.

Emily shared that her daughter was hit by a car. The bike she had been riding was crushed. Her daughter was not hurt by the hit or falling on the road. Her daughter said it felt like a small bump and then she was moved to the side of the road.

Another of Emily's daughters was about three and told her that the man had come back again. Emily panicked thinking someone had been in their apartment. When seeing how scared her mom was, she told her that it was "papa" and he wanted her to tell her mom that it was okay; that she was okay. (Emily's stepfather (papa) had passed away.)

During a funeral, her niece was very upset that she had been lied to. She was told her "Gigi" had died and had gone to heaven. When they asked what she meant, she pointed to the corner of the room and said that Gigi was there smiling at her.

Chapter 10

Poetry

"When he reached the place where the road started down the Mount of Olives, all of his followers began to shout and sing as they walked along, praising God for all the wonderful miracles they had seen."

Luke 19:37 NLT

"It's Not a Coincidence"

By Emilie Lancour

It's not a coincidence at all
It's the spirit, the Holy Spirit
Part of God invisible except
For the wind, flames, and the pure white dove
It's the spirit, the Holy Spirit
Acting through us as a sign of love
It's not a coincidence at all
It's all part of God's unfailing plan

A rainbow coming out after a long rain
The treasure found at a weekend rummage sale
A random Bible page is the perfect verse
Stuck in traffic and you avoid a car crash
You hit the snooze and awake to see the sunrise
The feeling that someone is always watching

You finally make a call and hear the news
Stopping at the store and getting a big hug
The forgotten keys and you notice the stove
Prayers are answered just when you think they won't be
Falling asleep before you finish the prayer
The songs on the CD are perfectly right

Poetry

After a blessing, the disease disappears
Visions of angels watching over the earth
A child falling asleep after mom prays
Seeing eleven-eleven on the clock
A flying pig drawn by someone who can't know
The email exactly when you need it most

The homily that speaks directly to you
A friend calling before you can call her
Light in the corner of your eye when you pray
A perfect heart appears in the precious Blood
Smiles from a stranger as you pass on the street
Memories of a loved one when you feel down

It's not a coincidence at all
It's the spirit, the Holy Spirit
Part of God, invisible except
For the wind, flames, and the pure white dove
It's the spirit, the Holy Spirit
Acting through us as a sign of love
It's not a coincidence at all
It's all part of God's unfailing plan

"Footprints in the Sand"

Author Anonymous

One night I dreamed a dream.
As I was walking along the beach with my Lord.
Across the dark sky flashed scenes from my life.
For each scene, I noticed two sets of footprints in the sand,
One belonging to me and one to my Lord.

After the last scene of my life flashed before me,
I looked back at the footprints in the sand.
I noticed that at many times along the path of my life,
especially at the very lowest and saddest times,
there was only one set of footprints.

This really troubled me, so I asked the Lord about it.
"Lord, you said once I decided to follow you,
You'd walk with me all the way.
But I noticed that during the saddest
and most troublesome times of my life,
there was only one set of footprints.
I don't understand why, when I needed
You the most, You would leave me."

Poetry

He whispered, "My precious child,
I love you and will never leave you
Never, ever, during your trials and testings.
When you saw only one set of footprints,
It was then that I carried you."

About the Author

Emilie Lancour is a mom to three young men and a daughter -in-law, an educator, an author, a nature photographer, and a writer. Family, friends, and faith are most important to her. She is an outgoing person who loves quiet time on the beach with God, her camera, and a journal.

After her husband passed away, she started a blog, grief-faithandfinances.com. In 2020, her first book, "It's Okay to Be Okay; Finding Joy through Grief" was published. This memoir tells the story of her healing journey and what helped her get out of bed each day.

Emilie, in addition to writing, takes nature photography, mostly of the beautiful Upper Peninsula of Michigan and Lake Superior. Her unedited photos can be viewed on Instagram @upuneditedphotgraphy.

Record Your Own

My Miracles

Record Your Own

My Miracles

My Miracles

Record Your Own

My Miracles

My Miracles

Record Your Own

My Miracles

My Miracles

Record Your Own

My Miracles

My Miracles

Made in the USA
Monee, IL
17 May 2022

96564733R00062